Why Dogs Have Black Noses

Elizabeth Laird

Illustrated by
Tianyin Wang
Chris Coady
Chris Vine

CONTENTS

RD
RESS

Dear Reader,

There are more than 400 million dogs in the world today and all of them are descended from wolves. Throughout history, people have used dogs to help them hunt, to guard their villages, to pull their sledges, and to round up their sheep. In modern times, dogs are often pets, or trained to work for the police, or to help people who have difficulty seeing or hearing.

People have always watched and wondered about dogs, noticing their special skills, their bravery, their curiosity, their sense of mischief and also their loyalty. Stories to explain these are found all over the world. Some of them are here in this book.

I hope you enjoy them!

Elizabeth Laird

Why Dogs Have Black Noses

A myth from Ghana

Back in the first times, when the world was new, the monkeys lived in peace and happiness. They had no enemies. They passed all their days swinging from tree to tree, deep in the forest, and eating the delicious fruits which hung from the branches. But they were curious about everything, just as monkeys still are today.

'I tried to talk to a warthog today,' one of them said, as they lay about in the trees one afternoon, munching mangoes. 'And do you know what, he refused to chat! All he said was, "I've been digging all day, trying to find roots to eat, and I've had to run away from a leopard. Go away, Monkey. I'm much too tired to start talking to the likes of you."'

'How rude!' said the others. 'Why did he speak to you like that? And what was that word he said? *Tired*? We've never heard it before. *Tired*. What does it mean?'

'Search me,' said the first monkey. 'I asked the warthog to explain, but he just curled up, closed his eyes and went to sleep.'

The monkeys chattered all through the lazy evening about this new word *tired*.

'Perhaps it means the same as hungry,' one of them suggested.

'Or happy,' said another.

'Or proud,' said a third.

'This is silly,' said the first monkey.

'Tomorrow morning, let's go and ask Nyame, the god of the sky. He'll explain.'

* * *

The next morning, three of the most curious monkeys trooped off to see Nyame.

'We've heard a new word – *tired*,' they said. 'And we've come to ask you what it means.'

The god of the sky smiled at the foolish monkeys.

'It's much better for you not to know,' he replied. 'Aren't you happy as you are? You have everything you want up there in your trees. Ripe fruits fall into your hands, and the branches are too high for even leopards to reach. Go away, monkeys, and be happy as you are.'

But the monkeys' curiosity was too great.

'We want to know!' they pleaded with Nyame. 'Tell us what *tired* means.'

At last, Nyame gave in.

'Very well,' he said. 'Come back and see me this afternoon. You'll find out then. But don't blame me if you're sorry afterwards.'

Chattering happily, the three monkeys
went back to their forest home, and waited
impatiently until it was time to return to Nyame.

When they were all in front of him again, the
god of the sky showed them three big boxes.

'Take these,' he said. 'Carry them out of the forest until you reach the wide grasslands, where there are no trees. Go far out across the grass, and then open the boxes. You'll find out soon enough what *tired* means. But I'm warning you, the lesson will be hard. Are you sure you want to learn it?'

'Oh yes, we do! We do!' chorused the monkeys.

* * *

The monkeys heaved, pushed and pulled the boxes through the forest until they reached the far side. They gazed out across the savannah lands, where not a single tree was growing. Nyame's words still rang in their ears, so they set about struggling with their load across the savannah.

An hour later, the monkeys could contain their curiosity no longer.

'This must be far enough,' they said. 'Come on! Let's open the boxes now. Let's find out what *tired* means!'

They prised the lids off the boxes with their clever little hands and peered into the boxes.

Enormous eyes glistened back at them. Then, with a terrifying growl, out jumped three huge, fierce dogs.

The monkeys leaped backwards, then turned and ran. The dogs immediately began to chase them. In their forest home, the monkeys could climb trees to escape from danger, but here, out on the wide yellow savannah lands, there were no trees.

The monkeys had to run.

They ran as fast as they could, but they had never run before. They were soon puffing and panting with exhaustion.

The dogs caught the youngest monkey, and then the next youngest, until at last, only one monkey, the very one who had first spoken to the warthog, was left alive.

Desperately he ran, his feet pounding the hard earth, his lungs bursting, his heart pumping furiously. At last he reached the edge of the forest. With a final burst of strength, he climbed up into the tree's welcoming branches and sat there, exhausted, shaking with fright.

Nyame, watching from above, saw that the lesson had been truly learned. It was time for him to act. Just as the three dogs reached the forest edge, Nyame pulled them to him and rubbed charcoal on their noses. This meant that they could not smell the monkey or see where he had gone. At the same time, he took away the dogs' ability to climb.

The monkey, when at last he had recovered his breath, slowly crawled from branch to branch until he came to where the rest of his family were sitting. 'Well?' they said, offering him a banana. 'Did you see Nyame? Did he tell you what *tired* means?'

'He didn't tell us. He made us find out for ourselves,' groaned the monkey. 'Oh, it feels terrible. I never want to feel like this again.'

And he flopped down into the crook of a branch and fell asleep.

From that day to this, all dogs have black noses, which Nyame stained forever with his lump of charcoal. And no dogs can climb trees, which is a great blessing for all the creatures that live in them.

Lenanu and the Gentle One

A Maasai myth from East Africa

At the beginning of time, the first dog was God's pet. He was called Lenanu, and heaven was his home. He followed at God's heels, and he and God talked together all the time.

In those days, heaven and earth were close together, and it was easy to go backwards and forwards from one to the other. Lenanu liked running down to earth, and most of all he liked the first man. He enjoyed playing with the first man's children, and watching the first woman with her baby.

One day, God said to Lenanu, 'I don't mind if you want to go and talk to the man, but you must promise me one thing.'

Lenanu looked up at him with his head on one side and his tongue hanging out. He was trying to look solemn and serious.

'I promise,' he said. 'Honestly. I'll do whatever you ask me.'

'It's not hard,' said God. 'I just want you to keep a secret. Don't tell the man about my Gentle One. I've given him everything on the earth, the plants and all the animals for him to use and hunt, but the Gentle One I've kept here for myself. If the man knows about her, he'll pester and pester me until I give her to him.'

'I won't say a word,' said Lenanu, and he thought he meant it.

But the very next day, when he was lying beside the man's fire, chewing on a bone which the woman had given him, he blurted out, 'If only the Gentle One was here! She's so soft, and sweet. I know you'd like her!'

The man pricked up his ears.

'Who's the Gentle One?' he asked. 'I've never heard of her.'

'Silly me,' said Lenanu. 'I'm not supposed to tell you. Still, now I've begun I'd better go on. I don't suppose God will really mind.'

And he told the man all about the Gentle
One, and how good it was to touch her, and
how easy it was to lead her, and how she was so
humble and quiet and pleasant.

'I like the sound of that creature,' said the
woman. 'Go and ask God, husband. I'm sure
he'll give her to you.'

'The Gentle One! The Gentle One!' chanted
the children. 'We want the Gentle One!'

* * *

The man went to God and began to beg and
plead and pester for the Gentle One. At first
God refused, furious that Lenanu had broken
his promise. But eventually, God gave in to the
man, and gave him the Gentle One to take back
to earth.

The man and his family were delighted.

'I'm going to call you Sheep,' said the man.

'And we're going to call your babies Lambs,' said his children.

But God was still angry with Lenanu.

'You gave me your solemn promise not to tell the man about my Gentle One!' he thundered. 'And you broke it!'

Lenanu was ashamed. He dropped his head and shuffled towards God with his belly in the dust and his tail between his legs.

'I'm sorry, I know I was wrong,' he said. 'Please forgive me. I promise I won't do anything bad again.'

'It's too late for that,' said God. 'How can I trust you now? You have broken your word. Since you like the man so much, you'd better live with him and be his servant. Your food will be the scraps he throws to you and whatever you can scavenge for yourself. Go away, and don't come back to heaven.'

Lenanu was sad. He didn't want to leave his comfortable home and fend for himself on earth.

'Father God,' he pleaded, 'if you're sending me away, please grant me what I need to survive. Give me a good nose, so that I can sniff out my food. Give me legs that are fast and strong to carry me quickly over land and help me swim through water. And give me whiskers, so that I can feel my way in the dark.'

God granted Lenanu's wishes. He was sad that his friend had betrayed his trust, but he wanted him to survive.

That's why all dogs, to this very day, can smell out food, and run fast, and find their way even at night. Perhaps that's also why dogs always

chase after sheep, because it was on account of
the Gentle One that Lenanu was sent away from
the comforts of heaven.

Why Dogs Always Chase Cats

A folk tale from the West Indies

Once, long ago, dogs and cats were good friends. One fateful day, however, Dog invited four cats to his house for dinner. There were the two brothers, Tatafelo and Stumpy John (called Stumpy because he had no tail) and their sisters, Finger Quashy and Jack-me-no-touch.

The cats were delighted with the invitation to dinner. They liked to sit in Dog's cool shady

• *Tatafelo:* (say) 'tah-tah-feh-lo'. **19**

sitting room and sip his tasty drinks. They liked the way he cooked his food, and they particularly liked the avocado pears, which grew on a large tree in his garden.

'Dinner with Dog!' Tatafelo said to his brother and sisters. 'How delightful!'

'And his avocados are ripe, I know,' said Jack-me-no-touch, who was the know-all of the family. 'I can see them from our house. They're shiny purple on the outside, and all soft and green inside.'

'Avocados! My favourite food!' purred Stumpy John.

Finger Quashy nodded and licked her paws, but she didn't say a word. Although no one knew it (not even her big sister Jack-me-no-touch), she was an expert thief.

'I've been up that tree every night after dark for the past two weeks,' she thought to herself. 'I'm sure I've eaten all the ripe avocados. What if Dog finds out they've gone and suspects me?'

After much waiting, the day of the dinner

came at last. The four cats brushed their fur until it gleamed. They washed their faces and trimmed their whiskers.

Dog was flattered to see that his guests had made themselves look so fine for his dinner. He welcomed them warmly into his house.

'He's being just as nice to me as the others,' thought Finger Quashy. 'I'm sure he doesn't suspect anything.'

'Well, dear Dog,' began Jack-me-no-touch, licking her lips, 'what are we to have for dinner this evening? Something delicious, I'm sure.'

'Some avocados, perhaps, from your fine tree?' said Tatafelo, twirling his whiskers with his paw.

'How lucky you are to have such a fine tree!' said Stumpy Jack. 'It's the envy of everyone around here.'

'Don't talk to me about avocados!' growled Dog, a ferocious scowl on his face. 'There's a thief around these parts. Every time I go out to pick a ripe avocado, I find that someone's been there before me. I've lost almost my whole crop!'

'How dreadful!' giggled Finger Quashy. 'Whoever could that be?'

'If I knew,' said Dog, 'I'd make them sorry, believe me.'

'It's that dreadful Rat! I know it is! It must be!' said Finger Quashy, her voice rather high and squeaky. 'He hangs around the place all the time, watching and waiting. He's the one, mark my words.'

She looked up at Dog through her long black lashes. 'Poor, dear Dog! How hard it is for you. You need a watchman. I feel so sorry for you that I'd do the job myself if you asked me.'

And all the time she was saying to herself, 'How silly this big dog is! He could never catch anyone as clever as me.'

'That's very kind of you, Finger Quashy,' Dog said, wagging his tail (which was a little awkward as he was sitting on a chair). 'I think I might take you up on your kind offer.'

'Let's talk about it after dinner,' said Finger Quashy. 'Is that burning I can smell? Coming from the stove in the back yard?'

Dog jumped up from his chair.

'My pots! They must be boiling over!' he barked, and rushed out of the room.

'I need to go to the bathroom,' said Finger Quashy to her sister. 'I'll be right back.'

She followed Dog out of the room. Peering in through the kitchen door, she saw Dog outside in the yard, stirring his pots over the fire he had lit there, and carefully adding salt and pepper to the tasty stew. But just by the window, sitting on a kitchen shelf, were two avocado pears all ready to serve to Dog's guests.

'Hmm,' thought Finger Quashy. 'This is easy.'

Before you could say 'dinner time' she had jumped up onto the shelf, and snatched up the two pears.

She was just about to jump back down again, when to her horror she saw that Rat was sitting under the shelf, watching her.

'Dog! Eek! Dog!' squealed Rat, as loudly as
his little voice would go. 'Come quick! A cat is
stealing your avocado pears! Eek! Eek!'

But Finger Quashy was too quick, even for Rat. She had already jumped out of the window, with the avocado pears clutched in her paws. In a flash, she threw them behind a bush, and dashed back into the sitting room. Calmly, without a single hair out of place, she picked up her drink, and began to sip it delicately through a straw.

A minute later, the cats heard a furious roar coming from the kitchen, and then Dog burst into the room.

'Which one of you was it?' he barked, glaring at his guests. 'Don't try to hide the truth from me! My last two pears are gone!'

'Are you accusing us of being thieves?' said Tatafelo extending his claws. 'How dare you!'

'What a way to treat your guests!' screeched Stumpy John, angrily lashing his tail.

'I've never been so insulted in my life,' said Jack-me-no-touch, making for the door.

'How could you?' said Finger Quashy, pretending to cry. 'I – I thought you were our friend!'

'No one is a friend to thieves!' roared Dog. 'And if you think I'm going to give you dinner after this, you can think again!'

He rushed at them, one after the other, but the cats had had enough. They were out of the house and over the garden wall before you could say 'avocado pear'.

Dog barked after them. 'Thieves! I'll get you!'

But by this time the cats had climbed a tree, and Dog knew he could never catch them.

Furiously, he went back home. But that was not the end of it, because then he went out into the yard and saw that sparks from the fire had flown up to the thatched roof. Dog gasped as he saw his whole house engulfed in roaring, crackling flames. There was nothing he could do but watch until it was no more than a pile of ash on the ground.

'All because of a thieving cat!' growled Dog. 'A guest in my own house!'

* * *

And that is why a dog can never see a cat without chasing it and why a cat will always run away from a dog.

Pulling Together

> *An Inuit legend from the Arctic*

Oki was the finest young hunter of his people. He could run like the wind and carry great loads on his back. He could pull fish from the coldest sea, and there was no one who could paddle a kayak with such speed and skill.

Oki's older sister was called Anuat. She was restless and adventurous. She liked running out along the shore, hunting small birds and taking them home to eat.

'I want to see life!' she used to say to Oki. 'It's so dull here at home. I want to meet other people and go to far off places.'

Oki's little sister was called Puja. She liked being at home and helping her mother. They would cut up the meat which Oki brought home, cook it, and sew clothes from the animal skins.

One winter's day, when the sea was quite frozen over, Oki and the older sister, Anuat, went off over the ice towards some distant islands.

'A fox! Look there! I'll catch him if I can!' shouted Oki, and he raced away, as fast as a wind-blown bird.

The fox was fast, and the chase went on for many miles, but at last Oki captured his prey. Pleased with himself, he trudged back to the place where he had left his sister.

She wasn't there. He looked out over the frozen white world and called as loudly as he could.

No one answered.

Then Oki saw marks in the snow. There were long double stripes made by a sledge's runners, and between them were the prints of reindeer hooves. All around, the snow had been churned up, as if there had been a struggle.

'What can this mean?' he puzzled. 'Has my sister been kidnapped? Why are there prints of reindeer hooves between the marks of the sledge runners?'

Baffled, Oki went home, hoping to find his sister already there. But she hadn't returned. For days and days the family waited and hoped, but Anuat never came back.

Weeks passed, then months. No one talked about Anuat any more, but she was in Oki's mind all the time.

'I must find her. I must!' he said to himself.

Spring was coming now and the warm weather was melting the ice between the islands. Oki gazed out across the vast stretches of icy water. 'If Anuat is still alive, she must be far away,' he thought sadly.

But Oki was determined to find his sister.
He thought long and hard.

'When the sea freezes again, I will set out.
But how can I avoid hunger and exhaustion?
If only I could move more quickly over the ice.'

Oki thought back to the reindeer prints
between the sledge marks. The seed of an idea
planted itself in his mind. Was it possible? There
was only one way to find out …

The next time that Oki went hunting, he took
with him a sledge and some strong cords.

'Where are you going?' little Puja asked him.
'What are those cords for?'

'You'll see,' said Oki, and off he ran, pulling
the sledge after him.

It was days before he came home. From inside
their snow house, Puja heard a strange noise. She
ran outside to look and screamed with fright.

'Father, Mother! Oki's come home, and he's
brought a monster with him!'

Her parents ran to look.

'This isn't a monster,' laughed Oki. 'It's a baby

bear, and I'm going to train him to pull
my sledge.'

Oki's father shook his head and smiled at his
son's folly. Oki didn't care. He made a harness for
the little white bear and taught him to run ahead
of the sledge pulling it along behind him. But
the bear cub tired quickly and soon lost interest.
So off Oki went again.

A few days later, he came back. This time, unearthly howls brought Puja running out to look. She screamed even louder than before.

'Look at its teeth, and its great round eyes, and its horrid bushy tail!'

'It's nothing to be scared of!' scolded Oki. 'What a baby you are! It's only a wolf cub. Now let's see what he can do.'

Oki harnessed the bear cub and the wolf cub together, and tried to make them pull the sledge. But they fought each other, biting and scratching. They refused to make the sledge run at all.

Oki didn't give up. He made a special harness so that the two young animals couldn't reach each other. He petted them, and gave them good food, and at last he made them run together. But the wolf ran fast, and the bear ran slowly. The sledge went round in circles!

Oki tried again. He caught another wolf cub, and this time he trained all three to run together, with the bear in the middle. Now it was going well! Oki could ride on his sledge far and fast, and carry heavy loads, too.

* * *

Winter came again. The sea was once more frozen into a vast sheet of ice. The sun hung low in the sky, and night fell almost before it was day. Oki made a new sledge, stronger and faster than his old one.

'I'm going to look for my sister,' he told his parents. 'I won't rest till I've found her.'

His father and mother were worried.

'We've lost one of our children,' they said. 'How could we bear to lose another? Stay at home, son. Forget your sister. She is lost to us forever.'

But Oki was determined. 'I have my animals now to help me,' he said. 'We can cover miles and miles in one day.'

He set off, racing fast to the place where he had last seen his sister, out on the ice that covered the sea.

Soon, the bear was tired and slowed the others down, so Oki unhitched him and carried him on the sledge.

Now, with the wolves alone, the sledge shot

forwards, swishing across the ice faster than any person could run. On and on went the wolves, while Oki cracked his whip over their willing backs and shouted cries of encouragement.

And so they crossed the sea, until at last they came to the far shore where the ground was rough and uneven. It was impossible to run the sledge over it.

Oki hitched his sledge to an iceberg and gave each of his animals a big chunk of meat to eat.

Then on he went on foot, alone. He was tired
and hungry but he wouldn't turn back.

'I'll find you, Anuat. I'll find you!' he
muttered to himself through the freezing wind
that ruffled the fur edging to his hood.

At last, he came to a settlement of igloos. A
woman came out at his call. It was Anuat herself,
and in her arms was a baby, all muffled up in fur.

'Oki!' she cried, her face lighting up with
delight. 'How did you get here? How did you
find me?'

He followed her into her igloo, and the brother and sister talked long into the night.

'That day,' Anuat said, 'when you ran off after the fox, some strangers came past. They snatched me up and carried me away on their sledge. It was pulled by a reindeer, so we were soon far beyond anywhere I had been before. I fought and struggled, but they wouldn't let me go.

'Eventually we reached this land and I was forced to stay. But then I met a good kind man here. We fell in love and married. Look, we have a baby now! There was only one thing that was making me unhappy, and that was the thought of my family, worried and wondering where I was.

'Now you have come all this way to find me! But how did you do it, Oki? How did you come so far across the sea ice, on your own?'

'I'll show you in the morning, if you'll come down to the edge of the sea ice with me,' said Oki, yawning. 'But now, dear sister, I want something to eat. In fact, I want a feast! So let me see what's in that pot bubbling so hard on the fire. I could eat a whole seal all by myself!'

And from that day to this, people have used the descendants of wolves to pull their sledges across the frozen Arctic landscapes.

Here Come the Dogs!

A folk tale from India

The dogs all around Jamal's village were barking like crazy one evening.

'What's going on?' Jamal said to his uncle, who was putting up the shutters on his shop, ready to go home to supper. 'Are they trying to warn us? Are the bandits coming to attack the village?'

'Bandits? Of course not,' said his uncle. 'The dogs are barking at their age-old enemies, the jackals, that's all. They're reminding them not to get too big for their boots.'

He finished fixing the padlock on the door.

'I tell you what, Jamal,' he went on. 'Let's walk home together and I'll tell you all about it.'

This is the story he told.

* * *

Once upon a time, he began, there was a very proud jackal, who thought he was better than everyone else. He was big and strong, and a cruel bully.

'Me first! Get back, all of you,' he would say, whenever the jackals were running together. 'I'm the leader here. You've all got to do what I say.'

If anyone tried to stand up to him, he would nip them with his sharp teeth until they yelped with pain.

The other jackals hated the bully, but none of them dared to stand up to him.

One day, a cheeky young jackal found a bundle of papers lying on the ground outside the village. They gave him an idea.

'I'll have some fun with these,' he said to himself.

He picked the papers up and trotted over to where all the other jackals were sitting in the shade, waiting for the cool time of the evening when they could go hunting.

'Listen, everyone,' he said. 'We're the best of all the animals, aren't we?'

'Yes, we are,' nodded all the other jackals.

'And I'm the best of the lot of you,' said the proud jackal.

'Yes, you are,' said the others, looking at him nervously.

'We all know that,' said the cheeky jackal. 'So I think you should be our king.'

But as he spoke, he turned his head away to hide his smile.

The proud jackal looked around, very pleased indeed at the suggestion.

'What a good idea,' said all the others, wondering what all this was about.

'If you're going to be our king, you need some papers to prove it,' said the cheeky jackal. 'And I've just found the very thing. Hold them in your paw all the time, in the way that important people do. They will show that you have the right to rule us.'

'Yes, yes!' the other jackals said. 'You'll look really important and educated, just like a king.'

But more of the jackals were smiling now. They were beginning to understand the cheeky jackal's idea.

The proud jackal took the papers and tried to hold them in his paw. He had to tuck up his front leg to keep them against his chest. He hopped around on three legs, wanting to look as important as ever, but he looked so silly that all the other jackals had to stifle their giggles.

'You know what?' said the cheeky jackal. 'Kings have crowns, don't they, and beautiful robes and shiny jewels. You need to wear something special that will show everyone that you're our king.'

Now all this time, a fox had been lying nearby, watching what was going on. He didn't like the proud jackal, who had often chased him away with a sharp nip. Now he decided to get his own back.

'Take a look over there, on the rubbish pile by

the village wall,' suggested the fox. 'There's a yellow basket. If you shut your eyes and squint a bit, it looks as if it's made of gold. Why don't you tie it to your king's back? He'll look magnificent then.'

The proud jackal frowned at him.

'What's your game, Fox?' he growled suspiciously. 'Are you trying to trick me?'

The fox opened his eyes wide.

'Who, me? Trick *you*?' he said innocently. 'Now why would I do that?'

Two of the jackals were already tying the basket to the proud jackal's back, while the others stood around, pretending to look at their new king admiringly.

'Oh, Your Majesty,' they said, bowing low to hide their giggles. 'You look so royal! So grand! So ... so ...'

'So stupid,' the cheeky jackal muttered so quietly that nobody else could hear.

* * *

49

Over in the nearby village, the fox saw some dogs, lying by a wall.

'Three cheers for the King of the jackals!' he shouted. 'All together now, hip hip, hurrah! Hip hip, hurrah! Hip, hip, hurrah!'

The jackals all joined in, barking and yelping and howling at the tops of their voices. They made such a noise that the monkeys in the forest nearby chattered with alarm, and the crocodiles in the river slid beneath the water, and the peacocks by the mosque folded up their tail feathers and swooped away across the fields.

And all this time, the fox was watching the

entrance to the village, ready to run.

Then, just as he expected, the village dogs began to bark. The sounds of the jackals had woken them from their afternoon sleep. Their ears pricked, and they sprang up.

In one barking mob, they raced towards the jackals.

The jackals saw them coming. There were big dogs and little dogs, old dogs and young dogs, spotted dogs and plain dogs, all running out of the village as fast they could, ready for a fight.

'Quick, all of you, run for it!' the fox shouted to the jackals. 'Here come the dogs!'

The jackals didn't need to be told twice. They knew what the dogs would do to them. They ran for their lives, and bolted down the hole that led to their underground den.

Soon, there was only one jackal left above the ground. It was the new King of the jackals.

'Help me! Help!' he was yelling. 'I can't get down the hole! This basket's too big! I'm stuck!'

'Oh, the dogs won't hurt you,' the cheeky jackal called up to him. 'Show them your papers. Tell them you're our king. They won't dare to touch you then.'

'But dogs can't even read!' the King of the jackals shouted back.

'Neither can you,' said the cheeky jackal, feeling very bold now.

'How dare you! I'll get you for this! I'll ...' yelled the King of the jackals.

They were the last words he ever spoke. With snapping jaws the dogs were upon him, and soon they had torn him to pieces.

Down in their den, safe at last from the bully, the jackals waited until the dogs had gone back to the village. Then off they went to hunt for their supper, feeling very pleased with themselves.

* * *

'It's a great story, Uncle,' said Jamal, as he reached the door of his house, 'but how do you know that the dogs are barking at the jackals? Perhaps there aren't any jackals out there at all and they're really barking at bandits.'

'Listen, Jamal,' laughed his uncle. 'The dogs have stopped barking now because the jackals have all gone off to hunt. Don't worry, if the bandits come, the dogs will bark to warn us. Then we'll have to think of a way to outwit them, just like the cheeky jackal and the fox outwitted the cruel bully.'

Gelert, the Prince's Hound

> A legend from Wales

Long ago, there lived a great prince in
Wales called Llywelyn. The thing he
loved best in the whole world was to play with
his young son. He liked to throw the baby up
into the air and hear him shout with laughter.
His second favourite thing was to ride out of
his castle at sunrise astride his prancing horse,
leading his pack of hounds, as the huntsman
sounded his horn and the deer bounded
ahead over the frosty ground to escape.

• *Gelert:* (say) 'gell-et'. • *Llywelyn:* (say) 'thl-well-in'.

One day, when the scent of the deer was strong and the dogs were restless for the chase, Llywelyn decided to hunt. He called his huntsmen, mounted his horse and looked over the hounds who were barking joyfully and straining at their leashes. He frowned. Gelert, the leader of the pack and the Prince's favourite hound, wasn't there.

'Where's Gelert?' he demanded.

No one could answer. No one had seen the great dog since the day before.

'We'll have to go without him,' said Llywelyn, a frown creasing his forehead. He spurred his horse forward, unwilling to delay the hunt.

* * *

At the end of the day, the huntsmen trotted back to the castle proudly bearing a pair of fine stags. The hunt had been a great success. As they approached the castle, Gelert came limping out.

Llywelyn stared down at him in dismay. The hound's eyes were wild, and red stains matted his coat.

Llywelyn leaped down from his horse and ran inside. A terrible suspicion made his heart pound with fear. Whose blood was smearing the dog's

coat, and staining his knife-sharp claws?

'My son! Where's my son?' he shouted.

He raced to the room where his little son should have been lying peacefully sleeping in his cradle. There was no sign of the child. The cradle was turned upside down, the bed clothes were torn, and it was clear that a terrible struggle had taken place.

'You devil! You murdering fiend!' roared Llywelyn, and raised his dagger.

Gelert looked up at him one last time, his eyes filled with grief and shock, and died.

Then Llywelyn heard a little cry. He lifted up the cradle, and there, quite unharmed, lay his son, holding up his arms joyfully to his father. Beside him lay the body of a gigantic wolf. The creature's skin was scored by the marks of a hound's sharp claws, and deep bites scarred its face.

'Oh, my faithful Gelert, what have I done?' cried Llywelyn. 'You saved my son's life, and I killed you for it.'

He carried Gelert's body out of the castle, and buried it in a place where all who passed by could see it and learn the story of the faithful hound. A pile of stones was set over the place where Gelert lies, and the castle was renamed Beddgelert which means, the Grave of Gelert.

The Hounds of Actaeon

A myth from Ancient Greece

Diana, the goddess of the moon, rode every night across the sky in her great white chariot, casting her ghostly light on the earth below. But when dawn broke she would go deep into the forest with her companions, the nymphs.

Diana liked to hunt. If she saw a deer leaping through the undergrowth ahead, she would snatch an arrow from her quiver and send it flying.

On one particularly hot day, when Diana and her nymphs had chased a cunning, swift stag without success, they gave up the hunt.

Tired, hot and thirsty, they stumbled upon a pool. It was shaded by trees and fed by a stream of crystal pure water.

Diana laughed and clapped her hands.

'There's no one anywhere near here,' she said. 'We're quite safe from prying eyes. Let's relax and bathe.'

At once, her nymphs shed some of their outer garments and plunged joyfully into the cool refreshing water.

But, even though she was a goddess, Diana was not all-seeing. She did not know that another hunter was indeed nearby. A young man called Actaeon, who also loved to hunt, had been out in the forest searching for deer that day. He had with him his prize hounds, a pack of dogs as fierce and fast as wolves, which he had trained to bring down even the most powerful stag.

Actaeon, too, had been unlucky. His hounds had gone off after a scent, and though he had tried, he had been unable to call them back. He had stumbled on through the forest alone.

Suddenly, Actaeon heard the sound of splashing water and laughter. His heart lifted.

'Water!' he thought. 'To drink and bathe in!'

Not knowing who was there, he crept up cautiously to the fringe of bushes that surrounded the pool. He parted them and looked through. The sight of the goddess, laughing with her nymphs in the water, was so surprising that he stepped back hastily, afraid of intruding.

Diana, with the sharp ears of a huntress, heard the rustle of leaves. She looked up and saw the young man's eyes staring at her, his mouth open in astonishment.

She cried out with rage. Sparks of fury shot from her eyes.

'How dare you!' she hissed. 'You, a mortal, standing there, looking at the goddess Diana.'

She scooped up some water in her hands and flung it at Actaeon. It caught him full in the face and dripped down his body.

'Tell the world what you've seen, if you can!'
she hissed. 'If you can!'

Terrified, Actaeon turned to run, but
something strange was happening to him.
His neck was lengthening. He was falling
forwards and his arms, no longer arms at all,
were turning into legs, while his hands had
become hooves. His tunic had gone, and in its
place was a rough hide, covered with a thick
coat of tawny hair. And his head! His head!
His mouth and nose were pushing outwards,
his ears were rising and from the top of his skull
horns were sprouting – long, many-pointed,
curved antlers.

'What, what –' he managed to gasp, and then could say no more. Instead an anguished bellow came out of his mouth.

In the distance, his hounds, still nosing on the ground for the scent of prey, heard the sound. They lifted their heads. They growled, the hair rising on their necks, then they took off, running like the wind through the forest towards the pool.

Actaeon heard them coming. He knew his dogs. He knew their speed and savagery. He had seen stag after stag fall to their powerful snapping jaws.

He turned and bounded away, crashing through the undergrowth, his long red tongue hanging out, his eyes wild with terror. The dogs came nearer and nearer.

'No!' Actaeon tried to shriek. 'Don't you know me? I'm your master!'

But all he could do was bellow.

And the hounds, not knowing that it was their master they were hunting, went about their deadly work.

Back at the pool, heartless Diana heard the horrible sounds which the hounds were making. She knew what they meant. She laughed her silvery laugh and went on bathing with her nymphs.

The Dog Who Brought Trees to Life

A legend from Japan

Long ago, there was a kindly old man in Japan whose chief delight was his dog. The dog's name was Shiro. The two of them enjoyed the gentle pleasures of the old man's cottage garden, tending the plants and feeding the birds.

One day, Shiro bounded as usual into the garden. He was about to chase the spirals of dust blown about by the wind, when he stopped, lifted his nose and sniffed. Then, with an excited bark, he scampered over to a patch of ground and began to dig, whining and wagging his tail.

'What's that you're doing, Shiro?' said the old man.

Shiro took no notice of his master, but began to dig more furiously than ever.

The old man looked into the hole that Shiro had dug and saw, to his astonishment, the gleam of gold. Carefully, he removed the rest of the earth, and lifted out a hoard of gold and silver pieces that twinkled in the morning sun.

'Bless my soul!' he said. 'Look at this, Shiro. We're rich!'

At that moment, he heard a shuffling sound by the fence. Looking up he saw his neighbour, squinting into the sun as he tried to see what the old man was doing.

'What's that you've got there? What are you doing? Got a secret, have you? I always knew there was something funny about you and that dog,' the neighbour said nastily.

The old man laughed.

'Funny? Yes, I suppose it is funny,' he said. 'Look at what Shiro has dug up! Gold and silver! I need never worry about money again.'

The neighbour's eyes shone with greed.

'Well, who's a lucky man!' he marvelled. 'Why don't you send the brute over here and see what he can find for me?'

The old man hesitated. He didn't like his neighbour, who was cruel and selfish. But he was too kind-hearted to keep his good fortune to himself, so he let Shiro into his neighbour's garden.

Then he went inside to wonder at his new-found wealth.

As soon as he had disappeared, the neighbour aimed a kick at Shiro's flank.

'Get on with it, then,' he growled. 'Make me a rich man, too.'

Shiro sniffed around the neighbour's overgrown garden and a minute later began to bark and scratch at the ground.

At once, the neighbour shoved him aside, and started to scrabble in the earth with his bare hands. But all he turned up was filthy slime, which stank and fouled his hands.

Furiously, he turned on Shiro, and picking up a spade which was lying nearby he attacked the dog, killing him instantly.

The old man, hearing his neighbour's snarls of rage, ran out of his house. He stared in horror at his beloved dog lying dead on the ground.

'Shame, isn't it?' said his neighbour. 'Not my fault. Branch of that old tree fell down on him while he was digging. Still, you must have got sick of his barking, on and on, all the time.'

The old man didn't say a word, but picked up

his dog and carefully carried
him home. He buried him
below the roots of the
old pine tree, where the
two of them had often sat in
happy times, snoozing in the
sun. Then he burned incense
there and laid flowers on Shiro's
grave, weeping salt tears of grief.
At last, worn out with sorrow,
the old man fell asleep. That night
the dog came to him in a dream, and
magically, the old man could
hear him speak.

'Cut down the pine tree
above my grave,' Shiro told
him. 'From the wood carve

a mortar for pounding rice. When you use the mortar, think of me.'

The next day, the old man did as Shiro had said. He took a branch of the fallen tree, and lovingly carved a beautiful mortar, smoothing and polishing it till it shone. Then he poured a cupful of rice into it, and fetched the pestle to pound it.

'There was no need to ask me to think of you, dear Shiro,' he said. 'I do so all the time.'

But then, as he looked, the rice began to change before his eyes! Each white grain was turning yellow! The old man picked them up, astonished at their heaviness.

'This is gold,' he said aloud. 'Pure gold! What a miraculous thing.'

The old man wanted for nothing now. For the first time in his life, he had plenty of food to eat and fine clothes to wear, and there was always money to give to the beggars who came to his door.

His neighbour, watching all this through narrowed eyes, was tormented with envy.

One day, he crept up to the old man's window and saw how the grains of rice turned to gold as they were poured into the mortar.

Unable to contain himself, he burst into the old man's cottage.

'More good fortune, I see,' he said, with a threatening frown. 'And you're keeping it all to yourself. Now that's what I call selfish. Lend me your mortar, old man. I could do with a bit of luck, same as anyone else.'

With great reluctance, the kind old man lent his precious mortar to his neighbour, feeling in his bones that he would never see it again.

He was right. For as soon his neighbour poured rice into the mortar, the pure white

grains turned to dust. Enraged, the neighbour flung the mortar into the fire. It burned up fiercely and was soon reduced to ashes. He swept them up, put them into a bag, and handed it back to the good old man.

'Here's your mortar, or what's left of it,' he said with a sneer. 'Shame, isn't it? Not my fault. A gust of wind must have blown it into the fire when I wasn't looking. Still, you won't miss it. You've got enough gold to last you a lifetime, I shouldn't wonder.'

* * *

That night, as he lay on his bed, the old man whispered into the night,

'Come and talk to me again, dear Shiro. You have no idea how much I miss you.'

Shiro came to him once more in a dream.

'Take the mortar's ashes,' he told his old master. 'Scatter them on the dead tree that has withered in the corner of our garden. You will see something wonderful, I promise you.'

The old man did as Shiro said. When the

ashes of the mortar touched the withered tree, he watched open-mouthed as the dead brown leaves shuddered and turned green. Then shoots sprouted from the bare branches and flowers burst forth. The birds flew to the tree again and sang.

The old man nodded solemnly.

'This is a miracle,' he said, 'and it's one I will share with others.'

* * *

The old man set out from home, the bag of ashes in his hand. Everywhere he went he sprinkled them on dead and dying trees. People gasped with astonishment as the trees sprang back to life, and the old man walked on happily, leaving in his wake orchards full of fruiting plums and cherries.

His fame spread, and soon a prince heard of the old man and his miraculous ability to bring dead trees to life. The Prince called him to his drought-stricken garden, and soon enough all his trees, that had once been dead, were bushy and

green again. The Prince heaped riches on the old man who, tired out, but happy, returned home to live out the rest of his days.

His wicked neighbour, hearing about the miraculous ashes, scraped about in the fireplace for any that remained on his own hearth. Then he set out too, hurrying to the palace of another prince, hoping for a great reward. But when he scattered the ashes from his bag, the trees grew even more sick, the dry leaves fell off, and the branches cracked and fell. Not only that, but the ashes flew into the eyes of the watching Prince and nearly blinded him.

'Seize that man!' the Prince cried out, clutching at his painful eyes. 'He's an imposter! Catch him!'

The old man's neighbour was punished and he

returned home with nothing. The good old man nodded when he heard about this.

'This is your doing, dear Shiro,' he whispered. 'You have brought happiness to me, and justly punished my neighbour for his cruelty and greed. Now you can rest in peace.'

The Dog and the Rice

A legend from China

When the world was very young there was a terrible flood. All the people had to escape up the mountains as torrential rain flooded the plains below.

At last the rain stopped, and the swollen waters began to go down. First of all a few humps of muddy land appeared, and then a few more. Soon the land between the humps became visible and the people began to recognise their land again. They were very relieved.

'We can go home again,' they said. 'Remember all the fruit we used to pick from the trees and the vegetables we grew in our fields? It will be so good for things to go back to normal.'

But they were wrong. Things did not go back to normal at all. The fields were still marshy and the water never properly drained away. All the old plants the people had eaten before the flood had died under the water and turned to rotten brown mush.

For a while, the huntsmen kept everyone fed. They went out day after day and came home with skinny rabbits or a few small birds. The food was carefully shared out. There was just enough to keep people alive, but their bellies were never really full.

It was a dog who came to the rescue. He was a curious animal, always exploring and trying out new things. He wasn't afraid to paddle in the remaining marsh land and sniff about for whatever he could find.

One day, when he returned to the village, he ran up as usual to his human friends with a cheerful bark.

'What's that hanging off his tail?' a farmer said. 'Goodness, that's a sight I haven't seen for a while! Look, they are fine fat seeds. I wonder ...'

He pulled the seeds gently from the dog's tail and planted them in his old field, which was still marshy. They grew into healthy plants, and when the farmer's wife had cooked them, the family sat down to eat their first ever helping of rice.

The rice filled their bellies and the people knew that they need never be hungry again.

Ever since then, people have been grateful to dogs for the gift of rice. And that is why, when the rice harvest is brought in from the paddy fields, the dog always gets a good share of it, too.

Why Dogs Have Hairy Coats

A myth from Siberia

There was a time when the world was empty. There were no great forests of trees, stretching from horizon to horizon. There were very few animals, and they were not as they are now. The dog, for example, had no hair on his body, and his skin was bare and smooth. There were no men or women at all. They had yet to come into being.

It was the great god Ulgan who created the first man and woman. He made the man first, moulding him out of mud, mixing it with water so that he could model a human form. He rolled out the clay to make a body, then a head, and he shaped arms and legs, with toes and fingers added on.

'How will this creature make children, if he doesn't have a wife?' thought Ulgan.

And so he took a rib from the man, and from it he made a woman.

The man and the woman lay lifeless on the ground. They were perfect in every way, from the crowns of their heads to the soles of their feet, but they did not yet have living spirits. They could not breathe, or move, or think, or speak.

Ulgan wanted to find spirits for the people he had made, but he did not dare leave them lying alone and unguarded on the ground. He called the first dog to his side.

'Look after my new creation,' he said to the dog. 'I don't want any harm to come to them while I'm away.'

The first dog sat beside the motionless people. The sun went down, and as night fell, he began to shiver.

'If only I had something to keep me warm,' the dog said to himself. 'If Ulgan hadn't asked me to keep watch over these strange creatures, I could at least have crawled into a hole, out of the wind.'

Now there was another god in those days, called Erlik. He was a cunning trickster and was jealous of Ulgan's power.

Erlik always had his ear to the ground, ready to make mischief wherever he could, and he heard the first dog complaining of the cold.

In an instant, he was sitting on a rock nearby, smiling across at the shivering creature.

'You poor thing,' he called out soothingly. 'No one should be outside on a night like this. Come over here, little dog, and I'll give you a nice warm coat.'

The dog looked longingly at the god, whose form was dim in the shadows.

'I can't move from here,' he called back. 'Ulgan has asked me to guard these people. He has gone to find spirits to bring them to life.'

'Ulgan?' scoffed Erlik. 'Why should you care about him? Did he offer to give you a coat to keep out the cold, as I'm doing? What has Ulgan ever done for you?'

A particularly chilly blast of wind came whistling through the trees as he spoke, making the first dog shiver so hard that his teeth chattered together.

'Do you r-really have a c-coat for me?' he said. 'Couldn't you b-bring it over here to me?'

'Oh no,' said Erlik. 'If you want it, little dog, you must come and get it.'

'If I stay here without a coat, I'll die of cold,'
the first dog thought. 'Anything's better than
that, even if Ulgan does beat me when he finds
out what I've done.'

So he stood up and trotted over to the rock
where Erlik was sitting. Erlik held out a coat
of thick brown hair. The dog put it on. He was
so busy wrapping the soft warm coat around
himself, and pulling it on over his four paws,
that he didn't notice Erlik slipping across on
silent feet to where the man and the woman lay,
spiritless, in the dust.

'So this is what Ulgan has been doing,'
thought Erlik. 'He's made these creatures and
now he must be off to look for spirits for them.'

Erlik raced down to the edge of a lake nearby
and picked a hollow reed. Then back he came,
and leaning over the humans, he blew through
the reed into their nostrils, bringing to life first
the man, and then the woman.

'Ulgan may have made you, but I gave you
life,' he told them. 'I am the father of mankind,
not him.'

The man and woman sat up, rubbed their eyes
and looked round in wonder.

The first dog was still admiring himself in his new coat.

'It's so warm!' he thought. 'A bit tickly, perhaps. I'll keep it for these cold nights and take it off during the day, when the sun is high.'

He ran back to the humans, ready to stand guard once more, but was shocked to find them standing up and walking about.

'Oh what have I done?' he barked. 'Erlik has tricked me! How could I have trusted him? And what will Ulgan say when he comes back?'

He didn't have long to wait. Ulgan's mighty footsteps were already shaking the ground as he strode back to his creation.

When he saw that the man and the woman had already received their spirits and come to life, he wanted to lift his great arm and strike them dead, returning them to the mud from which he had made them. But the first frog, watching from the shallow water, croaked out, 'Let the people be, Ulgan. If they live, let them live. If they die, let them die.'

Ulgan accepted the frog's advice, but he turned his fury on the dog.

'For what you have done, you will be punished,' he told him. 'That coat you wear will be stuck to your skin forever. You will not be able to take it off, however hot the sun. And you will live with the man and the woman and be their servant and their guardian for evermore. It will be up to them to treat you well or badly. If they are cruel to you, you will have no one to blame but yourself.'

Then Ulgan lifted his shaggy head and roared out, 'As for you, Erlik, you have interfered once too often. For what you have done, I banish you to the Underworld, and you will never see daylight again.'

From that time to this, the trickster Erlik has ruled over the Underworld. He crouches on his black throne, surrounded by evil spirits, who fly out when night falls to gather up the souls of the dead.

And as for the dog, he is condemned to live in his hairy coat, whatever the weather, and be at the beck and call of his human masters.